Blastoff! Readers are carefully developed by literacy experts to build reading stamina and move students toward fluency by combining standards-based content with developmentally appropriate text.

LEVELS

Level 1 provides the most support through repetition of high-frequency words, light text, predictable sentence patterns, and strong visual support.

Level 2 offers early readers a bit more challenge through varied sentences, increased text load, and text-supportive special features.

Level 3 advances early-fluent readers toward fluency through increased text load, less reliance on photos, advancing concepts, longer sentences, and more complex special features.

★ **Blastoff! Universe**

Reading Level

Grade K

Grades 1–3

Grade 4

This edition first published in 2025 by Bellwether Media, Inc.

No part of this publication may be reproduced in whole or in part without written permission of the publisher. For information regarding permission, write to Bellwether Media, Inc., Attention: Permissions Department, 6012 Blue Circle Drive, Minnetonka, MN 55343.

Library of Congress Cataloging-in-Publication Data

Names: Mattern, Joanne, 1963- author.
Title: Cottonmouths / by Joanne Mattern.
Description: Minneapolis, MN : Bellwether Media, Inc., 2025. | Series: Blastoff! readers: slithering snakes | Includes bibliographical references and index. | Audience: Ages 5-8 | Audience: Grades K-1 |
Summary: "Simple text and full-color photography introduce beginning readers to cottonmouths. Developed by literacy experts for students in kindergarten through third grade"-- Provided by publisher.
Identifiers: LCCN 2024003109 (print) | LCCN 2024003110 (ebook) | ISBN 9798886870398 (library binding) | ISBN 9781644878835 (ebook)
Subjects: LCSH: Agkistrodon piscivorus--Juvenile literature.
Classification: LCC QL666.O69 M353 2025 (print) | LCC QL666.O69 (ebook) | DDC 597.96/38--dc23/eng/20240208
LC record available at https://lccn.loc.gov/2024003109
LC ebook record available at https://lccn.loc.gov/2024003110

Text copyright © 2025 by Bellwether Media, Inc. BLASTOFF! READERS and associated logos are trademarks and/or registered trademarks of Bellwether Media, Inc. Bellwether Media is a division of Chrysalis Education Group.

Editor: Betsy Rathburn   Designer: Brittany McIntosh

Printed in the United States of America, North Mankato, MN.

Table of Contents

Water Danger	4
On the Hunt	10
Growing Up	18
Glossary	22
To Learn More	23
Index	24

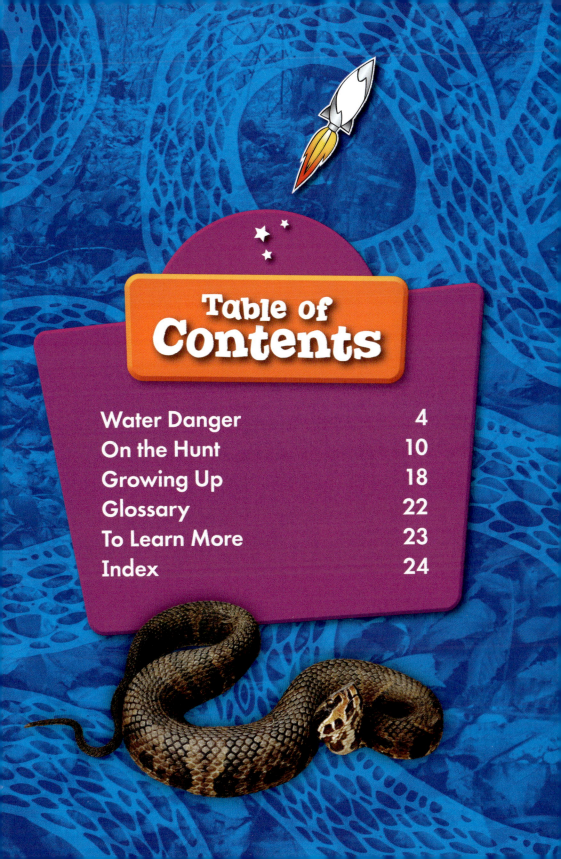

Water Danger

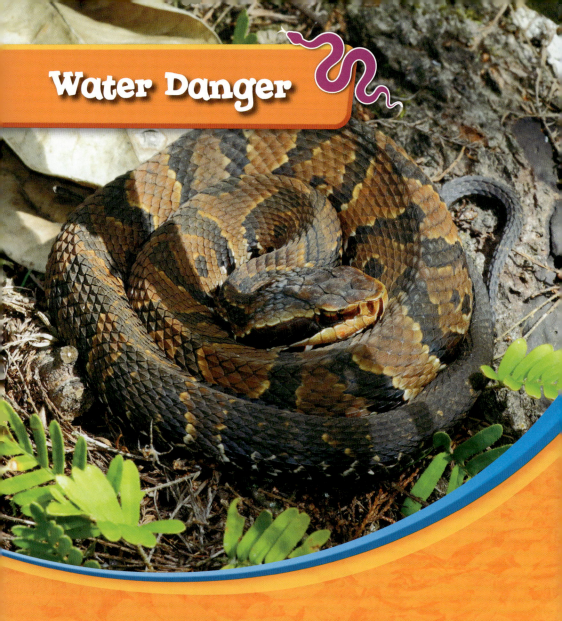

Cottonmouths are **venomous** snakes. They are also known as water moccasins.

They live in the southeastern and south-central United States.

Cottonmouth Range

range =

Cottonmouths are long and heavy. They can grow up to 6 feet (1.8 meters) long.

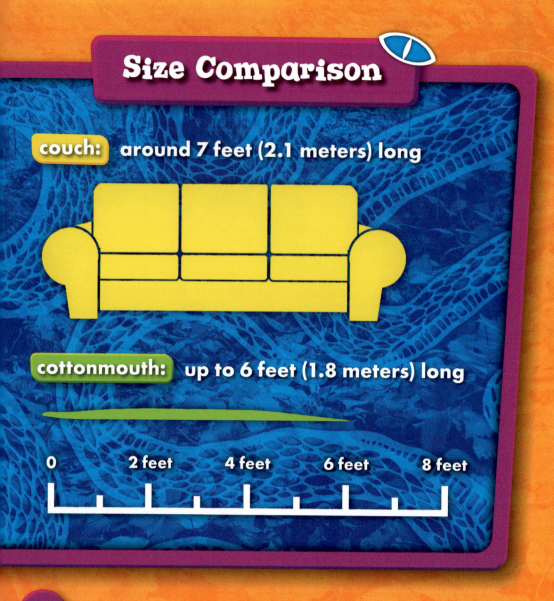

They weigh about 4 pounds (1.8 kilograms). Males are larger than females.

Cottonmouths have brown, dark green, or black **scales**.

The insides of their mouths are white like cotton. This gives the snakes their name.

Spot a Cottonmouth!

white inside mouth

long, heavy body

brown, dark green, or black scales

On the Hunt

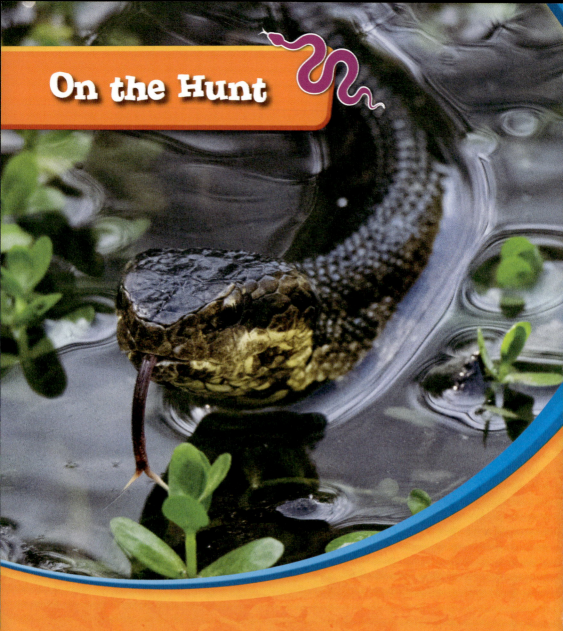

Cottonmouths live in **wetlands**. They look for **prey** on land and in water.

When it is warm, they **bask** on rocks and logs. In winter, they rest underground.

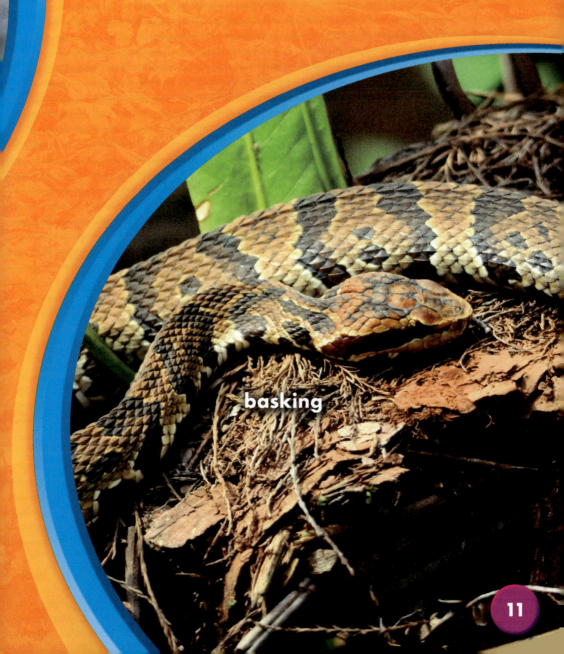
basking

Cottonmouths have **pit organs** near their eyes. These help them sense heat from prey.

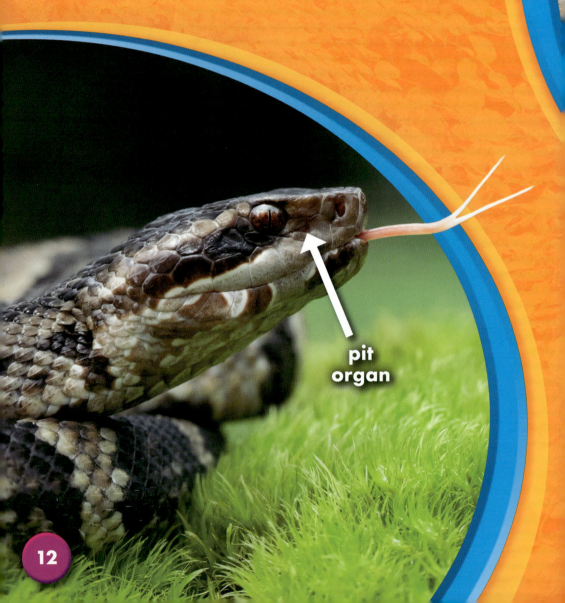

pit organ

Cottonmouths bite to release venom. Then they swallow their prey whole.

Cottonmouths are **carnivores**. They eat many different foods.

They often hunt fish and small **mammals**. Birds, frogs, and snakes are other favorite foods!

Cottonmouth Food

fish

small mammals

frogs

Few animals hunt adult cottonmouths. The snakes scare danger away.

They open their mouths wide and shake their tails. **Predators** stay far away!

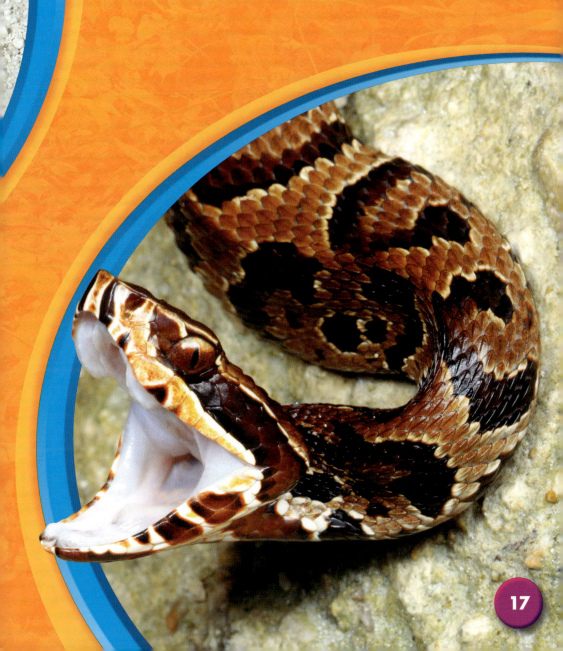

Growing Up

Female cottonmouths have babies once a year. They give birth to live young.

Up to 20 babies are born at once.

Young cottonmouths have yellow tails. They keep these for about a year.

The snakes grow quickly. Soon, they rule their wetland homes!

Cottonmouth Stats

status in the wild: least concern

life span: up to 24 years

Glossary

bask—to lay in the sun; cold-blooded animals often bask to raise their body temperatures.

carnivores—animals that only eat meat

mammals—warm-blooded animals that have backbones and feed their young milk

pit organs—body parts that help snakes sense heat

predators—animals that hunt other animals for food

prey—animals that are hunted by other animals for food

scales—plates that cover an animal's body

venomous—able to produce venom; venom is a kind of poison made by some snakes.

wetlands—areas of land that are covered with low levels of water for most of the year

To Learn More

AT THE LIBRARY

Albertson, Al. *Cottonmouths*. Minneapolis, Minn.: Bellwether Media, 2020.

Mattern, Joanne. *What's So Scary About Snakes?* South Egremont, Mass.: Red Chair Press, 2023.

Maurer, Tracy Nelson. *Cottonmouths*. New York, N.Y.: Crabtree Publishing, 2022.

ON THE WEB

Factsurfer.com gives you a safe, fun way to find more information.

1. Go to www.factsurfer.com.

2. Enter "cottonmouths" into the search box and click 🔍.

3. Select your book cover to see a list of related content.

Index

adults, 16
babies, 18, 19, 20
bask, 11
bite, 13
carnivores, 14
colors, 8, 9, 20
females, 7, 18
food, 14, 15
hunt, 14, 16
logs, 11
males, 7
mouths, 9, 17
name, 4, 9
pit organs, 12
predators, 17
prey, 10, 12, 13
range, 5
rocks, 11
scales, 8, 9
size, 6, 7
stats, 21

tails, 17, 20
United States, 5
venom, 4, 13
wetlands, 10, 20
winter, 11

The images in this book are reproduced through the courtesy of: Chase D'animulls, front cover; George Grall/ Alamy, pp. 3, 4, 16, 17; Rusty Dodson, p. 7; Gerald A. DeBoer, p. 8; Kyle J Little, p. 9; Jay Ondreicka, p. 9 (inset); Kevin McDonald, p. 10; noel bennett, p. 11; Mark_Kostich, p. 12; Dalene Capps/ Getty Images, p. 13; Paul S. Wolf, p. 14; Seth LaGrange, pp. 14-15; Aleron Val, p. 15 (fish); Liz Weber, p. 15 (small mammals); LorraineHudgins, p. 15 (frogs); Mark Kostich/ Getty Images, p. 18; Barry Freeman/ Alamy, p. 19; Andrew DuBois/ Alamy, p. 20; KF2017, pp. 20-21; negaprion, p. 22.